# TABLE OF CONTENTS

# ACKNOWLEDGMENTS

I am most grateful for the hundreds of encounters I have had with a heart of gracious love foremost. I have been instructed, informed, and to a greater degree than you may know, shaped by your conversations. Your afflictions, tales, and tortuous pasts have made me even more aware of why God loves you with an unfathomable, everlasting mercy.

The Bible tells of Jesus coming ashore, seeing you on the shoreline, and his heart bursting in compassion.

Because you shared your story, I know why.

Thank you.

# WHY ARE YOU STILL ALIVE?

# AUTHOR'S INTRODUCTION

If you have experienced a close brush with death, we have something in common; we are kin. We can both honestly say, "I should be dead now."

One of my earliest memories is laying on my Aunt Delores bed, fighting for every breath. I was an asthmatic and allergic to cats. In the early 1960's good asthma medicine had not been invented yet, or maybe it hadn't made it's way to rural Maine.

My aunt had cats, and every time we visited her, I knew I would fight to stay alive again.

It's scary to see death knocking at your door, the first time and every time. In my years of talking with people about "the deeper topics," I've found that most of us have almost died, at least once in our life. Perhaps you just experienced                    that.

I think you'll agree that the aftermath to the near-death experience is an odd twilight zone. Having skirted the reaper's scythe, we find ourselves in an indescribable nowhere's land in which we are filled with juxtaposing emotions and logic. We are delighted to still be alive, certain we should have died, guilty because we deserve to be dead, angry it happened, scared of it happening again, wondering if something supernatural saved us, yet sure it had to be just chance, embarrassed that we are going to have to talk about it, and proud we survived.

In addition to all the mixed-up emotions just listed, I believe the aftermath includes a cleansing, too, like a cool thunderstorm at the end of a hot summer day.

It's a time of resetting emotions, re-prioritizing agendas, and finding time that didn't previously exist.

While in a hospital bed or otherwise detained, you cannot do what you normally would. You must leave some activities undone. This means your boss and subordinates will have to figure out how to do everything without you. Someone else will pick up your work. Someone will make the meals, get the kids to school, and feed the dog. Someone else will run the board meeting and keep the machines going.

Suddenly, without intention, we are not as vital to the spinning earth as we might have thought. This is both disconcerting and cleansing.

Disconcerting because we *are* important, truly. We do important things, and some things will not happen while we are "stuck" in a hospital bed, rehab unit, or emotional support community. Some of us are worried about how this will impact our income; living paycheck to paycheck is real life for most of us. Right now, your situation may seem like the damage to your finances, career, family, and future health is unredeemable. Therefore, we can all agree your situation is disconcerting.

But, being forced to be unavailable in this post-near-death zone is cleansing, too. Without minimizing the tragedy, we can also give voice to the welcome rest. The reprieve is good. The break from the pressing needs of everyday life gives us a needed time of restoration. There is a mindset that says, "I have no choice but to sit in recovery, no choice but to let my body and mind settle and heal."

Can you find that perspective and sit in it? Can you let go of the "disconcerting," even momentarily, to take advantage of this special opportunity to sit and heal? You don't want to miss out on discovering some things in this unique post-near-death zone.

The following short stories are amalgamations of hundreds of interactions. Without disclosing names, identifiable backgrounds, and complete stories, I've taken pieces of real situations and blended them together to share three stories in which you will see yourself. Put yourself in their shoes, take their side in the dialogue and you will find your heart swelling, and your mind thirsting for new information.

If I could visit you right now, rather than telling you about someone else, I would ask you about your story. Your story matters. Your life, up to the point that you nearly lost it, has a beginning, a middle, and a near end.

Your near end is related to your beginning and middle. We would discuss all three, but we would get to the vital question, 'Why, in heaven's name, are you still alive?'

It's this question, why are you still alive, that I wonder most passionately about. In most cases, a tiny instance of time and distance made an infinitesimal difference between life and death. In other cases, the exact time and space placed you perfectly in death's crosshairs, yet something we can't explain happened to save you.

In either case, here you are in recovery. By all accounts, you should be dead. But you aren't. You are most certainly alive. For now.

Why? Why are you still alive?

For some of us, we'd like to talk about it. But, for others, we don't. It's spooky, shameful, embarrassing, involves the supernatural, or involves talking about the afterlife. Ugh. It's all those conflicting emotions and logic we listed earlier that keep us from wanting to dig deeper into the mystery and purpose of our own, fabulously personal, unique life.

So, allow me to make this easier on you. I'm not wanting to make this uncomfortable, not much anyway. I wouldn't let it get too painful if I were sitting with you. This should be mysterious, interesting, and fun to explore.

First, let's celebrate. You are alive!

And then, let's agree that you, and I, *may* have been living with a little less purpose than we could. We have a limited time in the sun, with no way to know how much longer, but if we are still alive, is there something we still need to do?

Let's take this interesting post-near-death zone and use it to reflect, think about your purpose, think *bigger*.

It's time to reset. To do a reboot.

**It's time to reset our opinions.** Think bigger. Our opinions tend to narrow our peripheral vision. Resetting our opinions opens the view. Maybe you don't know some things. That's okay, right? You don't have to be right about everything, do you? You've got room to stretch your mind, and you finally have some time.

**It's time to reset our joy.** Think bigger. Isn't it possible there's something that carries us above the deadlines, dishes, diplomas, and diapers to a place of abundant joy?

**It's time to reset our purpose.** Think bigger. You don't believe 'life sucks, then you die.' Deep down, when you take some time to listen to your own intuitive voice, you hear something else. Something more significant, meaningful, powerfully purposeful.

In the following stories, all three of our characters are like you. Your circumstances are different than theirs, but you'll find some common ground in each of them. And just as you are being encouraged to dig for gold right now, they were also encouraged to take time to reset their opinions, joy, and purpose.

Tim is a 20-year-old drug addict who found his way to the local Rescue Mission.

Dan is a Ph.D. in Physics; at 45 years old, he is confident he knows how the world works.

Marie-Claire is 92, living alone in her home and ready to die.

Let their stories get you thinking. Open yourself to the mystery, while the knock on the door is audible. It's quiet now. You can hear the knock. Answer the door and enjoy!

# Why
## Are
### You
#### Still
##### Alive?

# WHY ARE YOU STILL ALIVE?

# Tim—Thunder Under the Hood

I n my years at the Rescue Mission, there were common themes of light conversation. The weather was one; homeless people are subject to the elements in a way most of us are not. Other discussions revolved around basic needs—the next mealtime, available beds, free clothing, and social service office hours.

I was concerned about the immediate needs of those coming to see me on a Saturday morning. But my main interest was getting to the more profound questions of life. I greeted them, invited them to have a seat and engage in an interactive message.

My objective was to bring their minds to a place of peace, comfort, joy, and contemplation. It's only there that we can take a moment to reflect on life's deeper meaning. Why am I here? Not here at the rescue mission, but here on this planet. What's the purpose of living? What's the purpose of suffering? Is there really something beyond what we can see, feel, and touch?

These questions are personal. Not personal as in, we all have our own truth. Truth is truth— opinions don't change truth. But personal as in, we all have experiences that have shaped us and changed us; some of those experiences have cut deep scars and are hard to think about. The wounds are covered over, but it's crusty skin over a festering infection.

Some who sat with me on Saturday mornings might come back for many weeks. If they returned, it was because they enjoyed the messages of hope, love, and grace. They liked knowing they could speak their mind and be accepted, and it felt good to know somebody wanted to hear their story.

But Rescue Missions are transient places. On any given Saturday, I knew most were not going to be there next week. They needed a place to be for a few hours, lay their head down on the plastic table, and rest. They couldn't care less about me, my message, or my desire to engage with them.

If they were going to share at all, though, I found another common theme among the homeless—a story about a near-death experience.

"I should be dead," they would declare. Some with bravado, some with misty eyes. The stories they told publicly would raise the hair on the back of my neck. But, when I could get them alone and feeling safe to share, the accounts often had me weeping with empathy.

Life is tragic. For some, it's undeniably hellish. But for every single human being, life is tragic.

Don't misunderstand, life is joy, too. There is a path of blessed living that will bring joy over the tragic, around the tragic, amidst the tragic. It's a joy that is infamously difficult to describe, joy that Jesus told the woman at the well, "If you knew the gift of God, you would have asked for it." The joy Jesus speaks of is powerful, pervasive, and life sustaining, but it's never going to eliminate the tragic, it will carry you *through* the living hell.

Therefore, every human being will experience the unthinkable, the I-never-thought-*that*-would-happen-to-me."

"What makes you say you should be dead?" I would respond.

"Oh, you don't want to know, but trust me, I should have died many times by now."

I would probe just a little deeper, "Have you ever wondered why you are still alive?"

"Oh," they often responded, "I know someone upstairs is looking out for me."

This answer often gave me an internal chuckle because I was nearly always talking to someone who had long since thrown out religion as useless/wrong. (I live in New Hampshire, the least churched state in the US.)

So, officially, they may not believe in God, yet they thought someone upstairs was looking out for them.

Why this paradox? Over the years, I concluded that this question, 'Why are you still alive?' stirs something innate inside of us. This question pierces through the brittle 'I hate religion' stuff to get to the underbelly of existential worth. Am I so worthless that *nobody*, even the guys upstairs, cares about whether I live or die?

Activated by this question—somehow—we sense that *something* kept us alive, otherwise, as we already declared, we should have been dead.

It's that innate sense I want to get to. Frankly, I don't like religion either. Religious practice itself doesn't answer the all-important question—what is the truth about my worth? Am I worthless, a chanced split of unintelligent atoms?

As I ministered over the years to thousands of people on the streets and in the Rescue Mission, my heart agreed with their raw emotion: *Don't talk to me about religion. Help me. For God's sake, help me. I'm drowning. I'm self-destructing under the pain of people who have disappointed me, and the shame of disappointing others. I don't need religion; I need truth that will help me!*

One raw truth is that we all know there is *something* beyond the physical—something upstairs. True atheists are rare for a reason: only a few people haven't taken the time to be self-aware enough to hear their own voice over the roar of self-imposed reason.

Therefore, nearly all of us agree there is something we can't see, measure, or touch.
>We know it.
>>But we don't want religion.
>We know it.
>>But we don't want to be told what to believe.
>We know it.
>>But we don't want anyone to tell us how to live.
>We know it.
>>But we don't know how to describe it or put our finger on it.

I agree. I don't like talking about religion, or rules to live by, or church, or convincing anyone to believe in anything. I want to talk about real life. I want to pursue truth. I want to help people find purpose and joy beyond tragedy.

If tragic is all there is, 'life sucks, then you die,' it's game over for me. I'm not interested. But if there is purpose, truly meaningful, existential, life-fulfilling, joy-inducing, mind-expanding purpose, I want to find it and help others find it.

So, when they declare, rightly so, "I know someone upstairs is looking out for me," I repeat the question.

"You see," I say, "my question wasn't '*Is* there someone looking out for you?' Certainly, I agree with you that there is somebody upstairs looking out for you. But **_WHY are you still alive?_** Why did someone upstairs keep you alive? There must be a reason. You should have died by now, many times. Why, in heaven's name, are you still alive?"

When Tim asked me to be his mentor, he knew we were going to get to the big questions. Tim had come off the street as an addict a few weeks previously. He had progressed well enough to be accepted into the Discipleship Program where he had a guaranteed bed every night and was required to have a mentor. My objective was to help Tim become independent again. With sobriety, a successful attitude, and a stable job, he could move out of the Rescue Mission.

I invited Tim out to lunch to start our first mentoring session. We were at a new BBQ place on Main Street and the burnt ends brisket was to die for.

"Tell me a little about your childhood, Tim."

"Oh, I don't know, my childhood was like everyone else. I grew up here in Nashua. What about you, where did you grow up?"

Tim was a deflector. It was not easy to get to the truth of his childhood. Truth is truth. But some truth is so painful we can't readily look at it. Tim had hinted once on a Saturday meeting that his childhood wasn't easy. I was a patient listener, ready to hear when he was prepared to share.

His glasses were crooked on his head, a bit like his smile. His hair was always in bedhead condition. Not like a fashion statement, but like a real bedhead. He had a tick when he got nervous, a rise of his shoulder and a sweeping movement of his head. He tried to make it look intentional, as if he was just looking away, but it was a tick. Bone thin, his skinny arms had too many needle tracks to only be twenty years old.

Drug abuse is a topic of conversation that could consume hours of stories about how and why he started on drugs, but I wanted to get beyond the symptom to the underlying pain. I believe we *all* have underlying pain from something we perceive as tragic. Everyone has a different perception of tragedy, but tragic is in *every* life. Furthermore, we *all* have our methods of escaping from the underlying pain.

Drugs are an easily identifiable escape hatch; but there are dozens of others. Anger, dangerous sports, obsessive hobbies/work, eating topics, control topics, fear/anxiety, depression, sexual topics.

I'm not a professional therapist, just someone who cares, and knows another who cares even more. I have no judgment, I don't see any of us as better or worse, strong or weak. The simple truth may be that an addict needs to stop doing drugs, but I don't think that's helpful advice. I believe we need peace and joy in our life so we can stop the noise caused by the pain. And I believe everyone *can* grow closer to peace and joy, and moreover I am convinced *we all deserve it.*

We didn't get very far in that first meeting. But Tim and I continued to meet regularly for the next several months. We talked about many topics and slowly uncovered some of his pain.

It still makes me shudder to recall the depth of abuse he suffered. His mother had been trafficked as a young girl and sold from one pimp to another. She was originally from Atlanta and ended up in New Hampshire. She'd had three other children before Tim. Tim didn't know any of them.

Tim was taken from his mother by Child Protective Services at the age of three. Foster care was not great, but at the age of seven, things seemed like they might get better. His mother got clean long enough to win him back. He was happy.

But it turns out that bad men and drugs are a toxic cocktail for a woman who feels she doesn't deserve joy.

Tim showed me the cigarette burns on his arms and torso. His forearm was broken and never set, leaving him with a permanent bulge and arc to his arm.

But most of the scarring was internal. Tim said his tick showed up when he was fourteen. One of his mom's boyfriends locked him in the back shed. He got fed once a day and raped once or twice a week. The rats came up from the river behind the shed and crawled over him at night to get the crumbs. His mother never came looking for him. She had told him he was a child of hell, worthless, and would never be any good to anyone. Eight months later, just as winter set in, Child Protective Services found him and placed him again in foster care.

"Do you think that's true, Tim? Do you think you are a child of hell and worthless?"

He dipped a french fry in some catsup and scrunched it into his mouth. We had been meeting twice a week for six months. We would have a meal and then go to a local church for an evening music event on Tuesday nights. In addition to our one-on-one sessions, he was at my table every Saturday morning, participating in my interactive style of message—he had heard about the love of God the Father hundreds of times from me and others who were pouring into his life.

Tim had also become a daily Bible reader, devouring ten chapters a day, reading all the notes and cross references. He was making considerable progress in assimilating the messages of unconditional love from God. No rules, no judgment. Just relaxing and letting Jesus love him. He saw it all written down, everything he ever needed to know about mercy, forgiveness, and love. And he seemed to be developing a direct relationship with God on his own.

But, six months into his journey, I wondered if he was only getting head knowledge. It's great to know about God through reading the Bible and studying the meanings of the words. But until we fall in love, it's just an academic exercise. Academics isn't life transforming, only a love relationship transforms.

He looked up at me. His new glasses looked great on him. He had new clothes that fit, and his hair was combed.

His eyes started to mist. He rubbed his left eye with his crooked arm. "I mean, I know what God says. I believe I am hearing from Him when I read my Bible. I know He disagrees with what I was told by my mom and the men who abused me. But…"

He stopped, looked away and choked on emotion.

I waited for him to settle his raw feelings so he could finish. He fidgeted with a french fry, then picked it up and flung it at his plate.

"But, sometimes, I don't know. It's like I need to turn God's volume up loud enough to overcome the voices in my head that tell me I am worthless."

"It will come, son. I promise. Just stay steady. You didn't get hurt in a couple months, so it's going to take some time for you to live out your new faith."

"But what if I really am worthless? What if I'd *rather* be worthless? Sometimes I just want to go get a fix. It sucks. It's hard living this new life. Sometimes I wonder where the good news is?"

I handed him another napkin and he wiped his eyes.

"The good news is with you right now, son. He's all around you. The good news is living in you, and you are living in Him. I know the struggle, too. It took me years to fight the urge to drink. But I promise it will get easier over time. Just keep pivoting. Turn your body and…"

Tim interrupted me to finish my sentence, "I know, turn my body, and tell Jesus, 'Take this from me Lord. I can't do this on my own. I need your grace now.' I do. I pivot and declare many times a day. And it works. And I know He answers my cries. But sometimes I still hear *their* voices in my head. I feel the shame of sexual abuse, and the rats crawling over me. She was my mom; she was supposed to protect me. Why didn't she?"

"Tim, when you ask the Lord, what does He say?"

Tim sniffled and wiped his nose. "I have asked, and I believe He told me that His grace is sufficient for me. And the thing is…"

Tim put his head down into his hands and took another minute to get his emotions under control.

He looked up at me, "And the thing is…" His shoulders started to heave as another wave of emotion hit him. "…His grace *is* sufficient. It always is. He reaches out and hugs me. And He tells me to get up and keep going, *with* Him.

"But Pastor Randy," Tim continued, "I don't deserve His grace; I suck."

I looked at him and smiled, "I know, me too, which makes Him the perfect Savior for guys like us. We don't deserve His love; we said no to His love for years. And yet, here we are. He pursued you and me until we finally said, 'Okay, you can love me if you want.'

"And now look at you, devoting a part of your every day to loving Him back, listening to Him. The Bible says,

> *By your endurance you will gain your lives.*

*Luke 21:19*

"Look at the progress you've made. You know the words are written by eyewitnesses. You see the logic that proves He lived, died, and rose again, and that it couldn't be any other way to make sense of the historical facts.

"And you know how you have viscerally reacted to His words—the spontaneous tears of joy, even now. This is evidence that you've started to fall in love, Tim. You've experienced the pangs of a heart filled with the living water of grace upon grace. You've experienced it. It's real. It's truth.

"Stay in the love, Tim. You actually *do* deserve it. Let Him continue to change you. You'll come to *fully* believe He has great things for you. Like thunder under the hood of a Formula One race car, His voice is going to get louder and louder in your head, telling you that you are fearfully and wonderfully made, that you are loved with an everlasting, all-merciful love, that you were created in His image, to live in abundant joy as a royal priest in His kingdom. Maybe your mom's voice will still be there, even years from now. But you will come to believe God more than your mom."

He looked up and smiled. He stuck his index finger in the air. "Actually, I already do believe God more than my mom. I like the way you put that. I'm going to hold onto that. I **know** He is right, and nobody else is right. *I know that in my my soul.* When I hear my mom's voice telling me I'm worthless, I'm just going to tell her she's wrong!"

"I'd like to go back to my essential question, if that's okay, Tim."

He knew the question. He had already wrestled with it. And he knew it was one of the questions that I wasn't willing to fill in for him, insisting he had to find it in the Bible himself.

"Do you know *why* you survived the tragedy of your youth? Why are you still alive?"

Tim looked back down at the french fries. He took three of them together in his boney fingers, dipped them liberally into catsup and shoved them into his mouth.

He knew the question was coming. And lately he had been asking God and getting convinced the answer was coming. Eating the fries right then was a way of giving himself another minute to formulate the words out loud.

"Um. I think it's coming to me. Actually, I am 100% sure it's coming. I don't know exactly why I'm still alive. But I just know I'm going to know. I feel confident and hopeful. It's like this: I just trust that God has a plan. And I know His plan is going to be good. Probably sounds stupid, but I just believe it."

"Doesn't sound stupid at all, son. Sounds like God is doing His thing in you."

# WHY ARE YOU STILL ALIVE?

# Dan—Everybody's Got an Ism

I met Dan on a sunny autumn afternoon. He was sitting in the little park on Main Street, overlooking the Nashua River. He was taking a break from work. With a coffee in one hand, his arms splayed over the back of the bench, his head was tilted up at the sky like he was purposely harvesting Vitamin D from the sun.

I sat down on the bench and said, "Hi, I'm out offering prayer to people today. Is there anything I might pray about for you?"

He opened one eye and looked at me. He snorted a laugh. He closed his one eye again.

"Nooo," he said, "don't be silly. There is no god to pray to, so it wouldn't matter if you did."

"Yeah," I responded with my own chuckle, "I spent 50 years as an anti-Christian, so I get it. I might have agreed with you. Do you have any faith background at all?"

He brought his arms in and crossed them. He rocked his head forward and said, "Yeah, my grandmother went to church, and we went with her when I was a kid. But in high school I realized that physics explained everything I ever wanted to know about life."

He looked at me, ready to engage in confrontation. His eyes were bright, illuminated.

"No way," I said. "Me too! It was my senior year of high school, and my world suddenly came into focus. I took calculus and physics that year, and my mind was blown. The math of the trajectory and the shape of object in the trajectory all made sense. But honestly, I have said this to many people, and no one has ever known what I meant. You are the first person I've met who gets it."

We geeked out for the next ten minutes about our shared love for math and physics. Unlike me, who had gone on to a finance career, he had fostered his first love with a Ph.D. in Physics and was still in the field, working for a defense contractor.

Eventually we got around to faith again. I said, "So, what would you say if I told you that I could prove to you that it is illogical *not* to believe in the resurrection of Jesus."

"I'd say you are cracked. No way. And, I'd say bring it on. But, also, I gotta get back to work."

We made an appointment to meet at the local coffee shop the next day. He took a thirty-minute break at 2:30 every afternoon. And he said he would welcome the distraction from the intensity of his work.

The next day I met him and went through my logic.

"Okay," he said when I was finished, "I'm good with this. It's a clever way of looking at it. But I don't think you have scientific proof that Jesus was resurrected."

"You are right, nobody can scientifically prove an event took place. We can't repeat historical events, so there is no scientific proof. Remember, I didn't say I would prove the event happened. I said I would prove that it was illogical to say He wasn't resurrected. That is, all the logic lines up that He probably was resurrected. And to take the opposite side, you'd have to break with logic by denying historical facts."

Dan put his hand on his forehead. He rubbed it back and forth a couple times. Then he turned to the left and said out of the corner of his mouth, "Yeah, you did say that, and I agree the logic is good. I just don't like it. Something can't be right."

"Could be," I responded. "Maybe you can find it, I haven't been able to."

I changed the subject. "Hey, I noticed you walked in with a limp. What caused that?"

"I was in a bad automobile accident."

"Tell me about it."

"It'll have to be tomorrow. Same time?"

Dan and I continued to meet for several days at 2:30. He had thirty minutes every afternoon to walk to the coffee shop, get a cup of coffee, clear his head, and get back to his desk. I was a distraction for him.

At first, I assumed I was just a distraction from his work. His work was high precision math and physics. If he missed something, even by a micron, a part would have the wrong specs and the military jet/missile/whatever would crash. He couldn't tell me what he was working on—that's all I knew.

But it turned out I was a distraction from some other things that had already crashed in his life. We only had about fifteen minutes to talk each day. So, it took many visits to find out that over the last year he had lost his marriage, custody rights to his daughter, and his two best friends in the same automobile accident in which he was hurt.

"Dan, I am so sorry. You've had a year from hell, haven't you?"

"Yes," he responded, "and funny you would phrase it that way. The biggest reason I don't believe in God has little to do with science vs. the supernatural. I can't understand why we go through this hell fire. I'm not the only one who had a year from hell. How about the people who are starving to death while we sit here? I don't get it. If there is a God, why doesn't he stop this stuff from happening?"

I looked at him with compassion. He was right to question. On the surface it makes no sense.

"Dan, I agree, and applaud your question. But would it make a difference to you if you knew the answer? In other words, if I told you the answer would you believe me, and would it change your mind about God?"

"Hmmm…let me think about that. Gotta run. And I want to hear the answer tomorrow."

The next day I refused to tell him the answer as revealed in the Bible.

"Look, Dan, I don't believe people like you and I value answers from other people. You and I don't really believe other people. We need to discover it for ourselves. We must get back to the source material, recreate it in the lab, and come to our own conclusions."

Dan sipped his coffee and smiled. "You are right. I wasn't going to believe your answer. I mean, I like you. You aren't the average pastor, priest, or whatever you are. And I like our chats. But being honest, I was never going to believe you."

"Dan, there is a place where you will find all the answers. One day, you'll read it for yourself. In the meantime, let me ask you a question."

I put my cup down and turned my chair at an angle so I could stretch my legs. "Have you wondered why you are still alive after your accident?"

"No."

"It's an essential question of life, don't you think? Why did you survive, and why didn't your two friends?"

"I can't go there." Dan looked at his watch hoping the time was up. It wasn't.

"Why is that?"

"My friends were amazing people. Far better humans than I. I don't deserve to be alive; they do."

"I agree you don't deserve to be alive," I responded. "Better yet, God agrees with you. The Bible says that none of us deserve to be alive. And yet, some of us are *still alive*—you and I for example—and others aren't. So, there *is* a reason why you and I are still alive, but it isn't because we deserve it. Why do you suppose that you are still alive?"

Dan shrugged his shoulders. "It's all random chance. Some molecules collide and others miss."

"Hmmm," I returned, "not according to your first answer. If it was all random chance, as a scientist you wouldn't feel guilty that your friends *deserved* to live yet didn't. These two answers cannot coexist logically."

Dan smiled. "Okay. I agree. Obviously, I haven't thought much about this. What's the answer? Why am I still alive?"

I smiled back. I was silent.

"You aren't going to tell me, are you?"

"Dan, you wouldn't believe me even if I did. I think you need to read it for yourself. When you are ready, you'll read it."

Dan looked at me, confidence beaming from his eyes. "I don't think that'll ever happen."

"Perhaps you are right. But there will come a day when the answers in life seem foggy. It happens to all of us, Dan. Today, I know you feel certain that you'll never find anything but fairytales in the Bible. But you don't know that scientifically. You've never read it at all, much less read it with the unbiased mind of a true scientist, one who is willing to discover the unknown.

"But that's okay, because in due time we all come to a place of curiosity, usually when life doesn't make as much sense as we thought. It's in those moments we have two choices: head towards the mystery and discover the unknown, or give up, whither and die. You strike me as a fighter, Dan."

We continued to meet for several weeks. Not every day, but when I could fit it in. Our friendship was growing. I enjoyed his sharp mind and our inclination to challenge each other. He liked to text me little cartoons that made fun of Christians and I returned quips about his religion, Atheism. I had told him, "Everybody's got an ism, my friend."

One week he told me he had been promoted to management. And he was thrown into a thorny situation, trying to lead a group that had already given up on finding answers to the problem they had been assigned.

"You've said the Bible would give me the answers to every situation in life. I challenge you. Tell me where to go in the Bible to solve my problem, and I'll read it."

I laughed out loud. "No way! The planet will go off tilt if you open a Bible! This is a book you swore you'd never read! Are you serious?"
"Yup. Hit me with it. I'm ready."

"Okay. Go to Nehemiah and read slowly and carefully. Do **everything** he does. Everything he says, prays, everything. Don't skip anything even though you think it doesn't relate to your situation or your faith. Find a way to fit every one of his words and actions into your situation, even praying his prayers despite no faith. And let me know."

Within weeks, under Dan's leadership and Nehemiah's inspiration, the team was jelling and making measurable progress. Dan was pleasantly surprised. He agreed the managerial method was applicable, even brilliant. But it was still no reason to believe in God.

One day he didn't show up at the coffee shop. He was never late; his day was highly ordered.

I checked my text thread to make sure we had the right day.

I texted him.

Nothing.

Two days later I got a call from a social worker at Massachusetts General Hospital. He was in the ICU and requested that 'his pastor' be called.

Dan had been in Boston presenting some findings at an international Astro-physics consortium. He had left the convention to a standing ovation and got lost trying to make it out of the city. Boston is famously difficult to navigate, but he hadn't turned on his GPS because he thought he knew where he was going. In south Boston, on a street he shouldn't have been on, at a time he shouldn't have been there, he got caught in the crossfire of two gangs.

I got to the hospital at the beginning of visiting hours the next day. He was still in the ICU, though the doctor told me that he should make a good recovery and would likely be discharged from the ICU the next day.

Unfortunately, he slept through the visiting hours, so I couldn't speak with him. I was asked to leave, but just as the nurse was ushering me out, I saw his eyes open, and his lips move.

I stopped the nurse and begged her to find out what he said. She left me in the hall, went back in, bent down, and listened. She came back to me and spoke the words that brought tears to my eyes, and still does as I write this.

"I want to know why I'm still alive. I'll read it cover to cover. I'm in."

# Marie-Claire— Perfect Peace

The town I live in has about 5,000 people. We have a small monthly community newspaper with a Faith column. This is unusual since only 2-3% of NH attends church. But it's a blessing, and as a local pastor, I am invited to write the column every few months.

Marie-Claire came to church one day because she had read my entry in the newspaper that month.

After the service, she told me she wanted to meet, and asked if I could come to her house that week.

She lived in an old rural farmhouse on the far end of town. She greeted me warmly and ushered me into the living room where she had tea and biscuits waiting.

We chit-chatted for a few minutes, but it wasn't long before she wanted to get down to business.

"At 92, I have questions."

"I'm sure you do. What can I help you with?"

She took a sip of tea from her rose-covered teacup. The tea set was her great, great grandmother's from Quebec.

"I want to know if I'm going to heaven. I've been thinking about dying, more and more. Not much else to think about at my age."

"Well, what do you think? Do you think you are going to heaven?"

"Yes, I think I might. I was baptized when I was an infant. That was by a Catholic priest, but I haven't been to mass or confession for thirty years. I don't like what went on with the scandal—you know, I don't want to say it out loud. But so, I don't know if I'm going to heaven."

She looked at me like she had a plan: get me to tell her she was okay, drink her last sip, and show me out.

I wasn't surprised by the question. It is one of the more frequent questions I get, often about a loved one.

"Well, what's your understanding? What does it take to get to heaven? And by the way, do you really want to go?"

She looked cross at me, "Of course I want to go to heaven. I sure don't want to go to hell!"

"Well," I said with a smile, "I was just checking, Marie-Claire. I meet a lot of people who don't even like God. They would hate heaven; being with a bunch of people who are worshipping God 24/7 might be worse than hell to them.

"But, okay," I continued, "so you are certain you'd like to go to heaven. What is your understanding of how to get there? And do you think you qualify?"

She looked at me over the rim of her glasses. This wasn't going quite like she had planned. She wanted a quick answer.

She flung her words at me, "I have been a *very* good person. Everyone I know has already died, but they would have told you, I am a giver. I've never murdered, stolen, coveted, or any of that stuff. And I married one man, George."

She then hastened to add with a tilt to her head and an insistence in her tone, "As a *virgin*, I married him. And I was always faithful to him.

"We couldn't have children, so I volunteered my time at many charities and in our church, on their Boards, directing all the good that we were doing.

"We gave away a lot of our income to help others. Sometimes I gave away more than I should; but I believed I should give until it hurts. At times we truly sacrificed for others who needed help.

"But I've just been diagnosed with cancer, and it's got me thinking a lot. I don't *feel* sick, and the cancer is treatable, so I've decided to fight it. But still, it makes me think about death, particularly at my age."

"I am sorry to hear this Marie-Claire. I am sure this is making you think about a lot of things. Can I just say you look to be in terrific shape for 92. You certainly don't look anywhere near death, Marie-Claire. But I understand how things like this can make us start to ask questions about life after death. I am glad you are questioning, and I am honored you invited me to talk about it."

She smiled briefly and then rolled her hand in a gesture of 'Get on with it, answer my question.'

I said, "So getting back to your concern about where you are going after death, can I ask you another question? What's your relationship with Jesus?"

Marie-Claire once again gave me a little scowl. "I went to church most of my life. Sixty years Catholic, and five years Protestant. I think I ticked that box, nicely, don't you?"

"Well," I responded, "yes, if the box was church attendance, you seemed to have knocked that one out of the park."

She smiled proudly.

"So, can I ask, who is Jesus to you, personally?"

Her smile disappeared quickly. Marie-Claire was not pleased with my questioning. "Look, I don't understand what you are asking. You are making me more nervous than when we started. I just want a straight answer. Am I going to heaven or not? You are a pastor, right?"

"I am so sorry, Marie-Claire. I'm trying to be helpful. Yes, I'm a pastor, but you are asking a question that is above my pay grade. In the kingdom of God, I am just a servant. I'm in marketing and education. I'm not in management. There is only One in management who can say if you are going to heaven. Have you asked Him?"

She looked down at the teacup in her hands. "I guess I have. In a way, yes. I've prayed about it. But I'm not getting any assurance from Him. That's why I'm asking you."

"Well, Marie-Claire, let's look at what you've told me so far. You clearly are a good person. You've done a lot of good things in your life—probably way more good than bad. But, as some atheists accurately point out, nobody needs to be a Christian to be a good person. There are lots of people who do good things. And the Bible tells us that being good doesn't get us to heaven."

She scowled. I hurried on before she could say anything.

"You've been a good church goer, too. Which means you probably believe in Jesus. But the Bible points out that Satan also believes in Jesus. Satan isn't going to heaven just because he believes in Jesus, and neither are you or me.

"So, I asked about your *relationship* with Jesus. How close are you to Jesus? I know you don't want Jesus to tell you,

*"I never knew you; depart from me.'*
*Matthew 7:21-23*

"So, allow me to ask the question differently. Are you a daily Bible reader?"

"No," Marie-Claire said. "Definitely not. The Bible is written by men, about men, and about a male God. I'm a woman, and I lived through the Women's Liberation Movement. I don't need men telling me what to believe."

She had heard many things about the Bible, told them to me, and concluded, "I love Jesus, but I would never read the Bible."

"Can I ask one more question?"

"Yes." Marie-Claire looked at me with her chin raised in the air, like she was braced against the wind.

"Are you peaceful in your life? At 92 you've lived a long time. You've seen a lot. When you lay down to sleep at night, are you peaceful? When you think about your last years of life, are you at peace with what's ahead?"

Marie-Claire's eyes misted, fell, and she looked away. "No. I am not at peace. You turn on the TV and everyone's angry. I lay down to sleep, and I can't sleep, or I go to sleep and can't stay asleep. I wake up to loneliness, live in

loneliness and lie awake at night in loneliness. I wonder if I've been good enough. To be completely honest, I think about finding someone who will end my life early. There's nothing left to live for—it's stupid to keep living."

I reached across and took her hand in mine. I silently prayed for her while I spoke.

"Marie-Claire, perhaps peace is the best place for us to explore right now. Let's forget about heaven for the time being. Jesus said He came to bring us joy. In fact, He said abundant joy, in this lifetime. Jesus came to bring the kingdom of heaven, not to be confused with heaven after we die, but the *kingdom* of heaven to live in right now. He said to repent, which is to change your mind about Him, and believe He is the King of the kingdom, and those of us accepting His invitation live in His kingdom as His loyal subjects.

"He said, 'Follow me.' But most people don't know Him enough to follow Him. They don't take the time to get to know Him. Would you consider getting to know Jesus?"

She withdrew her hand, though not abruptly. She was softer in her demeanor. She smoothed her skirt. "What do you mean, get to know Jesus?"

"The Bible says the Word is with God, is God, and that Jesus is the Word. That means that Jesus equals God, who equals The Word. The Bible, therefore, despite what we might think of it, claims to be Jesus/God. Would you consider changing your mind, and reading the Bible *as if* it is Jesus?"

"I don't know. This is a lot to take in."

I reached over and took her hand once again. "I agree. How about I come see you again soon and we can continue to explore the topic together?"

Marie-Claire placed her other hand on mine and squeezed. "I'd like that. Thank you."

It turned out we couldn't meet for a few weeks. The cancer treatments had made her sick and she was sleeping a lot.

My next visit was on a sunny autumn day. The maple leaves had turned bright orange and red. Something was dying, but with a vibrancy only God could muster.

She seemed older. She was walking slower, a little closer to the ground. She met me at the front door and walked me to the living room. She was silent until we were seated for a few minutes.

She listed her grievances with disdain. She had so little energy she couldn't keep the house up. She was behind in the laundry, was not hungry most of the time but even when she was, she didn't have the energy to cook. She'd gone on Meals on Wheels, but the food was not like what she would cook.

She concluded, "This is no way to live."

"I'm sorry, Marie-Claire," I responded with sincerity. "Do you regret making the decision to fight the cancer?"

"Regret? Maybe. But I felt I needed to."

I was silent, assuming there was more to her story in explaining why she made the decision. However, she filled in the silence with something I didn't expect.

"Regret is a haunting emotion. There is a lot I regret in my life."

Sometimes, people need to confess their sins. During the fifty years I was an anti-Christian, I remember two times that I unloaded on a willing ear. Neither time was to a clergy or to a close friend, just someone willing to listen. I *needed* to get my regrets off my shoulders. The weight bogs us down. Jesus encourages us to let him take our load, that He came for the sinners, those in need of a physician, those who are burdened and heavy-laden.

Marie-Claire was heavy-laden, and she unloaded her burden on me that day. She'd suffered sexual abuse by her cousin, from the age of eight to twelve years old. He was eight years older and forced himself on her frequently. She was too ashamed to say anything. It stopped only because she got pregnant at the age of twelve. Her family had money and had her "go to a doctor to take it away." The cousin's abuse was finally exposed, though, and forced to stop.

She hated her story, because she had to lie that she got married as a virgin—she never talked about it, even with her late husband George. It was a secret she couldn't reveal. The shame was too deep.

Just as our own history affects us, her past had festered in her like an emotional cancer, silently growing and eventually showing up in multiple ways.

She slowly listed the ways her past had ruined her adult life.

She was a brutal wife, belittling her husband right into his early grave. She drank too much, and when she was drunk, she was even more abusive. She was distrustful, even calling herself paranoid, which alienated friends and family. George's side of the family stopped visiting early in their marriage.

She knew this about herself for most of her 92 years but had never admitted her failings to anyone until that day. In fact, she said, many had tried to counsel her, but she shut everyone down, unwilling to admit her shortcomings.

This was the reason, she told me, that she had gone to church—out of shame and a desire to be a better person. But, in her own words, "Church didn't make me a better person; I have always been hard to like."

She had one last confession.

"I do not like men." She looked at me and smirked. "I think the 'man's world' is what is wrong with this planet. And I do not like that men have one thing on their mind."

She looked at me, lifted her nose, and glanced at my waist. She couldn't say it, but her meaning was clear.

"But" she continued, "I have to admit I have not treated many men kindly. I have regrets about that."

She told me a few detailed accounts of some men she owed an apology to, though they were long since deceased.

That day was a lengthy visit, but I could see she felt relieved to share her burden. We made plans for me to come back.

I returned the next week, and she had the physical strength for me to take her out to lunch at the little café overlooking the Piscataquog river in the village of New Boston.

"Marie-Claire, I asked if you had peace in your heart about these last years of life. And you said you didn't."

She interrupted me. "I've thought more about this."

She paused. I thought she was going to say she had changed her mind and was at peace now.

"I may have had brief moments of enjoyment, but I don't know if I have ever felt peace for a day in my life. If my mind has idle time, I replay the abuse in my mind, and I have sorrow over the baby that was taken from me and the children I never had because of it. I think about the stress of our world when I watch the news or read the newspaper. I think about a conversation that irritated me, and I run through in my head everything I should have said or will say the next time I speak to them. I can't remember a day when I experienced peace.

I nodded my head. "I see, Marie-Claire. I'm sorry you are experiencing this."

I paused to let the sincerity marinate.

"What do you think about making it your mission to find peace over the next few years before you die?"

She looked into my eyes. "What do you mean?"

"Well, you've only got a few more years to live. It could be fifteen more years, but compared to your lifetime, it's only a few. What if we make it a mission to find peace for you?"

She looked away. "I don't want to live another fifteen years; I'd be 107. But anyway, I get your point. Yes, I'd like that. I want to find peace."

I opened my Bible. She noticed, and said, "I have heard about the peace of God and never understood it. Is that where you are going?"

"Eventually, yes, but before we can get to the peace *of* God, we must find peace *with* God. Here is the scripture,

> *Therefore, since we have been justified by faith, we have peace with God through our Lord Jesus Christ.*

59

*Romans 5:1*

"Marie-Claire, the Bible answers everything we ever needed to know about living a blessed life. And yet, Jesus said that few find the narrow gate. That's because the instructions for finding it are only heard by those "with ears to hear." Jesus doesn't want everyone clamoring at the gate if they aren't there on the right terms. His instructions are obtuse for those who only want something selfish, a ticket to heaven, a miracle, or to be fed with physical food.

"Allow me to give you the first three clues in finding the gate to peace. You can see in this first scripture that faith is a key that unlocks peace *with* God. The implication is that *we are not at peace with God before we have faith*. That is, before faith, we are at war with God. Being at war with anyone, let alone God, is not good soil for sowing peace. Most people don't think of themselves as being at war with God, but the Bible says that everyone without faith is indeed at war with Him. Empirically, we find it true because everyone who gets through the narrow gate looks back and agrees, "Oh, I see it now! I *was* at war with God!"

Marie-Claire was leaning forward in her chair, hanging on every word. "I am with you so far. But if faith is so important to finding peace with

God, how do if find faith? I mean, I already believe in Jesus."

"As you might imagine, the kind of faith God references isn't a simple 'belief in,' but a complete trusting that comes from an active abiding relationship. It's inconceivable to have strong faith in somebody you don't know. So, you must build faith by developing a relationship with Him. Here is the second clue:

> *So faith comes from hearing, and*
> *hearing through the word of Christ.*

> *Romans 10:17*

"Simply put, you'll find true life-changing faith by reading the Bible. It's the hearing of the word of Christ (Christ is the Word), that will bring faith, and sustain faith. It's not a wonder why the Bible is the bestselling book of all time. Billions of people have read it daily and found the same thing: life-changing faith.

"Lastly, let me share the final clue in unlocking joy-inducing peace in your life."

> *You keep him in perfect peace whose*
> *mind is stayed on you, because he trusts*
> *in you.*

> *Isaiah 26:3*

Marie-Claire was still leaning forward like she had heard that the keys to unlocking the doors of life were available, that the answers were coming, and she was ready to pounce on truth and wrestle it to the ground. "That's what I want, right there. Perfect peace. That's it. I want that! But *how* do I get that? I still don't understand what it's saying."

I smiled. "It's an odd term, but a mind stayed on God is a mind that is thinking about God, God's ways, and God's words frequently throughout the day. You could do any number of things to stay your mind on God. For example, taking one scripture with you each day and replaying it in your mind throughout the day is one method to keep your mind on Him. There are other ways, too; something will come to you."

Marie-Claire tilted her head and said, "But, so, the scripture ends with 'because he trusts in you.' Is this related to the faith you described?" She was sharp, I could see why she was a successful Board member in earlier years.

"Yes, indeed. Taking all three together, we see that faith, the all-trusting, the *I-am-all-in* kind of faith, brings us peace with God and a perfect peace. And our part is to read/hear the Word of God and keep our mind stayed on Him and His ways."

That day Marie-Claire decided to try. She was both excited and skeptical. Her reasoning was appropriate, "I've got the time. And this is something I've always wondered about. I've never understood the Christians who read the Bible every day. But at 92, if I will ever try to find peace, it's now. Will you help me?"

Marie-Claire died 14 months later. She survived the cancer, but the following winter she fell on the ice, broke her hip, and never recovered.

Peace did not come immediately to Marie-Claire. She had wrestled with people, and God Himself, for her whole life. But slowly, as she read the Bible daily, she started to find a rhythm that was not hers.

One day she said, "I feel like God is writing on me. It's like He's writing a new hymn. I'm the hymn, but perfecting the words, meter, and rhyme takes some time. It seems my destiny is to be a glorious song of praise and thanks to God. Does that sound strange to you?"

It wasn't long after that she realized she was in love. The Bible says that God *is* love. Love is not something we can hold in our hands or pour into a test tube to distill the chemical properties.

Love transforms us. It's that simple to state yet infinitely complex to describe. Jesus used many phrases to help us see the ethereal, despite our handicap of having human eyes. One such description was God putting us through a second birth, this time spiritual, in which we now experience the love of God for the first time, and we come to desire it more than life itself.

I watched a miracle unfold in Marie-Claire's life in those fourteen months. She changed. People noticed.

Sometimes, I can't handle the emotions of watching God work. I have cried a lot since He asked me to work for Him. It's like having box seats at the playoffs, and your home team wins. But infinitely more profound.

The last time I got to see her was in the hospital. She was weak; she could barely whisper. I prayed over her, anointed her with oil, and kissed her forehead.

When I stood up and looked at her, she tried to speak. I leaned back down to get my hearing aid close to her mouth.

"I know why," she said.

She spoke slowly; it took effort to get each word out.

"I wasn't ready before, but..."

I waited patiently while she caught her breath.

"God wanted me to finally fall in love with him and give me a year of peace."

I straightened up and smiled at her. But she had more, so I leaned back down.

"I praise Jesus. I love Him so much."

She squeezed my forearm with the little strength she had left and took an emotional, stuttering breath.

"And I love you, too. Thank you."

She died peacefully ten minutes later while I held her hand.

# WHY ARE YOU STILL ALIVE?

# Your Story—
# Answers Are
# Coming

I can't be with you to hear your story. I wish I could.

I don't know what you have been through. I don't know how many close calls you have had or when the last one was.

Or maybe you feel you've never had a close call. But have you driven somewhere and not remembered how you got there? Because of intoxication, distraction, or fatigue, we arrive at our destination and don't remember part of the journey. We made it, but why are we still alive to talk about it?

Tim, Dan, and Marie-Claire found God's purpose, peace, and joy. Each had endured some tragedies and eventually got curious about the bigger topics of life. It's possible to develop curiosity without a precipitating event, but most of us need something that shakes us awake.

What are we being woken up to see?

Something bigger, deeper, and beyond our big brains that makes us realize how small we are. A love that forgives every flaw in our character, every mistake, every crime, and every mean word we ever spoke. A presence that sits and weeps with us after each tragedy and then helps us out of our retreated fetal position to stand and live again in this raw, sometimes cruel world.

God has a plan for us to live out our unique giftings with Him. His superior knowledge of you—who you are, what makes you tick, what will make you thrive—means that His plan is perfect for you.

I had many opportunities to click into the plan He had for me. But for fifty years, I refused the invitations. Every asthma attack, every accident, every hospital admission, and every near miss was another wake-up call, followed by the awkward post-near-death twilight zone, followed by…unfortunately for me…just a return to my previous life. God nudged me dozens of times to get curious about His plan for me. Until one time, I finally opened the book I swore I would never read and fell in love.

This is your story, though, not mine. It would be best if you decided what to do with this free pass you were given to stay alive. Are you going to inquire of "someone upstairs?"

Answers are coming. But you'll have to seek them. After reading these stories, you know my advice. I am pleading with you to get curious about *why* you are still alive and let your curiosity *lead* you to read the Bible for yourself today, *with* a humble request that God reveal Himself to you. You don't want to wait. Everyone who delays, including Tim, Dan, and Marie-Claire, wishes they had answered the call earlier.

I know what some of you are thinking about the Bible because I have used all the arguments ever uttered against the Bible. There isn't anything you could say that I haven't expressed myself—but I was wrong, and I can now show you how I was wrong.

In my defense, though, I feel I was misled for the first fifty years of my life. The Bible doesn't say what some Christians say it does. The list of misrepresentations is long, so I won't detail them now; you'll figure it out when you carefully read it yourself. Some, claiming to be religious, have sorely miss-spoken for God in words and actions. Don't listen to or follow Christians, *including me;* hear and follow Christ.

Without detailing the common misrepresentations of the Bible, let me at least give you my opinion of a theoretical *source of confusion.*

Western Christians have changed Christ's message to fit into our goalpost mentality. In the West, we are linear thinkers focused on achieving goals. A winning-oriented mindset is not bad; it produces results—it achieves breakthroughs in science, technology, and human capacity.

Therefore, while goalpost mentality is not inherently wrong in every arena of life, it isn't a good fit in "the bigger topics." Life itself is more fluid, complex, flexible, and ever-changing.

Furthermore, goalpost mentality can encourage a win-at-any-cost, the-ends-justify-the-means, or I-am-right-you-are-wrong approach. If crossing the finish line ahead of everyone else or being in the "right" group is important to us, we are putting our needs ahead of others, doing what we can to save ourselves from losing.

This is not what the Bible teaches. Indeed, it teaches the opposite, to put others first, to finish last.

The Bible speaks of heaven and hell as two opposite realms after death, enough to believe they are real, but frankly, little information is given and mentioned only occasionally. When you read it for yourself, you'll realize the Bible doesn't speak of some of what you've heard from Christians, including how you'll land in heaven.

The Bible predominantly teaches us to know God's will for us *today while we are alive*. Getting to know God's path for us and following Him as the King is not a simple goalpost; it is infinitely complex.

Therefore, it's not a wonder when people don't believe a Christian who is yelling a warning of hell. Intuitively, the goalpost story is too elementary to come from an all-powerful, all-knowing being. Just one look at the beauty of nature and the intricate cells of our bodies, and we are witnesses to fabulous complexity.

Rather than two simple goalposts, the Bible informs us of something different, a way, a path of life. Paths are not linear or finite; they have ups, downs, bumps, turns, sun, shade, deep shade, tunnels, rain, and beautiful vistas which skirt cliffs, meadows, and mountains. The Bible invites us to live along this path of blessed living, of joy that superimposes on the achievements won and lost.

God isn't simple minded, and Jesus wasn't a Westerner.

In the Bible, you will find your purpose, at every stage of your life, in every circumstance. A part of your purpose shifts and changes as you do, as the people around you change and your family's needs change. Listen carefully as you read, ask Him as you read, and you will know His will, your purpose in general and in that moment. He'll never leave you purposeless.

All along your journey, God loves *you* as you are, and He is pulling for you. He is on your side, wanting you to feel whole, loved, and joyful. He continually whispers encouragement, relentlessly running after you to nudge you in the direction that He knows will be best for you, given what's coming later on the path.

Jesus dangled the good news in front of a woman who had been misled by religious people. Paraphrased, Jesus said, "If you knew, if you only knew how amazing this gift of God is, you would want it. And you would ask for it. Right now." She did and became one of the most famous unnamed women in history.

But all this good news, love, encouragement, nudging, and joy is silent to most people. God rarely reveals Himself and His will to those who don't humbly ask. He still actively pursues us, but if we don't want to humble ourselves, sit at His feet and listen, He mostly lets us do our thing.

He has chased you down again, put this book in your hands, and is saying to you, "Deaf ears can be opened. Everything is possible *with* God. I am willing to open your deaf ears; are you willing to hear me? Will you open my Word and let me bring it alive for you? If you knew how good this gift is, you would want it."

God knows how big of a leap this is for some of you. But not a leap of faith; He isn't asking you to take a leap of faith. Just because you believe something doesn't make it true. Your opinions don't change reality. You may not believe anything good about the Bible right now. So, this isn't a leap of faith; it's **a leap of action.**

> *Draw near to God and he will*
> *draw near to you.*
>
> *James 4:8*

If you draw near to Him, He will respond by getting close to you. It's your move first, though.

Depending on how big of a leap this is for you to draw near to him, you could make it easier on yourself. If you feel the leap is huge and would be embarrassing for others to know, don't tell anyone who could give you a hard time. Quietly download the Bible on your phone. No one needs to know—this is personal.

While you read, pray for a true understanding of the Bible. Tell Him you want to know His real message. I often sing out loud to Him:

> *Make me to know your ways, oh God. Teach me*
> *your paths. Lead me in your truth and teach me.*
> *For you are the God of my salvation, and for*
> *you I will wait all the day long.*
>
> *Psalm 25:4-5*

The first half is begging Him to **make me** know His ways. And the second half affirms my patience; his message in the Bible will peel like an endless onion, glory by glory. In a hundred years, you'll still be peeling more revealing.

You were given another gift of staying alive for a while longer. I encourage you to spend it living, *in* the greatest journey, *along* the longest path of converged intellectual and spiritual challenges you could never have imagined, and *with* abundant joy. You have purpose written all over your life, for you were created in His image, zealous for...

Jesus wept over Jerusalem because they did not know the time of their visitation. Real tears were shed over tragic and rampant religiosity that deafened the ears of many citizens. Some knew, but most didn't know who had visited them.

You were visited many times in the past. This is one more gentle knock on your door. Jesus has wept over the times in the past when you looked away or looked casually.

He's saying to you,

"Now is the day,

Now is the time,

My dear child."

# WHY ARE YOU STILL ALIVE?

# Resources

You will find many willing to help you get the right resources. But if you want to start this journey under the cloak of silence, the information below may help you take the first steps. This is not an exhaustive list of advice in becoming a follower of Jesus, just a few words to get you started.

## What Bible should I buy?

If you've never read the Bible, your first question may be, "What should I buy?"

If you are already attending church, please ask your elders. You should get their advice first.

Otherwise, the answer depends mostly on your learning style and personality.

Bibles come in two basic translation categories, word for word, and thought for thought. Word for word is a direct translation from the original manuscripts of every word individually. Thought for thought is the scholars' attempt to interpret the thought conveyed by the original manuscripts and write it out for you in a way they think you'll understand it best.

I am a geeky person. I study now in a word for word translation (mostly ESV). Yet, I started in an NLT version which is a thought for thought translation. Frankly, even a geeky learner like me benefitted from a thought for thought Bible to get me started.

Having said that, though, if you are ultra geeky, don't hesitate to jump directly into a word for word translation. This includes ESV, KJV, NKJ, NASB, HCSB. All are in modern English except the King James Version (KJV)—some find the old English elegant; I can't read it, it's too distracting for me.

For most of us, though, don't get guilt-tripped into thinking you have to be a purist right away—there is plenty of time later to study every word, even in the original languages.

Therefore, for all but the most studious learners, I recommend you start reading using a thought for thought translation. This narrows the list to a few key translations, New Living Translation (NLT), New International Version (NIV), New English Translation (NET).

Every Bible version listed above was translated by teams of scholars directly from the ancient manuscripts. I own and reference all the above. My first Bible was the NLT Life Application Study Bible—one of the most widely sold Study Bibles. The notes helped me to see the message clearly and relate it to my life.

## Do I Read It on Paper or Phone/Tablet?

There is no power in the paper; the power is in the message of God. Therefore, do what is best for you and your learning style.

My first Bible was paper. It helped me to underline key scriptures that spoke to me and take notes in the white spaces. It was 2008, and I was fifty years old; paper book reading is what I grew up with. I was not adept at underlining, highlighting, and taking notes on an electronic document. If paper books are right for you, every bookstore carries Bibles.

I now study on a phone/tablet. I use a Bible software app (there are many, I use Olive Tree) in which I split my screen to read the scripture on the left and commentaries or Greek/Hebrew/English interlinear references on the right. I've adapted to electronic highlighting and note-taking. Plus, I love having my Bible immediately available everywhere I go. Many Bible software apps include free downloads of Bibles. If electronic reading seems right for you, go to your app store, and find something you like.

## Where do I start, and how much is enough?

Again, you need to know your learning style. Geeky learners who are highly committed once they start a project would be fine starting in the beginning and reading through to the end. I did. If you do this, using a Study Bible is even more important—it's easy to get lost in the Old Testament without scholars helping you understand the context and historical background.

Otherwise, start at the beginning of the New Testament, in Matthew. Finish the New Testament, then go to the front and read straight through.

You should plan to read for thirty minutes daily, or about four chapters daily. At this pace, you'll finish in one year.

What about daily devotionals and watching Christian TV? These can be good *additional* ways to keep your mind on Him, but they are *not a substitute for "hearing by the Word of Christ."* Remember, Jesus said, "Follow me," not Christians. There are many great devotionals and preachers, but you don't need to learn from them as much as you need to learn from God Himself. It's God's Word that you need. Read it, fall in love, and live it. Your life is about to explode with love, joy, peace, forbearance, kindness, goodness, faithfulness, gentleness and self-control (the fruit of the Spirit, Galatians 5:22-23).

## **What about church?**

Again, knowing yourself is important. If you are introverted, anxious, and don't like crowds, it's okay to hold off for now. Take your time, *relax*, keep reading every day, and *let yourself* fall in love. God will have you wanting to go to church soon.

Otherwise, choose several churches and try a Sunday at each. You'll find a church to call home. Once you do, plug in.

There is no magic in any denomination, a particular church, or service style. The power is in God, not a people group. Ultimately you are looking for a church that believes in and actively, humbly teaches the Bible. It's that simple.

## <u>Other Books by Randy Loubier</u>

100% of book sales support direct ministry. I take no salary. Amazon is the easiest place to find my other books. www.randyloubier.com may also be helpful. If you can't afford a book, email me.

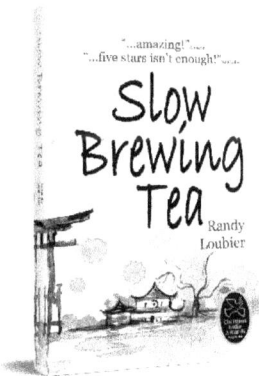

A finalist in the 2022 Christian Indie Awards, this novel is set in the remote mountains of Japan and will take you on a personal journey of discovering love, both human and divine. A young airman takes a motorcycle adventure though northern Japan in search of romance, God, and an understanding of the mysterious culture.

The second novel in the Slow Brewing Tea series. Maria boarded the airplane to leave her monochromatic life behind, begging for meaning, fire and adventure. Soon, she found herself enmeshed in Japanese prophecies that started 400 years ago with the great samurai, Oda Nobunaga, but now certain to become a revolution in modern day Japan.

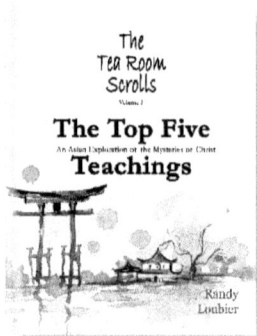

Mankind has questions—about the purpose of life, the path of blessed living, the way to live in peace, the pursuit of abundant joy. The Tea Room Scrolls is a mindful adventure through scripture that you will never forget as you ponder Jesus' answers to the most important questions of life. Volume 1, The Top Five Teachings.

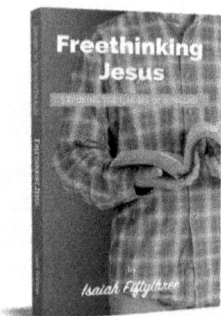

Written to people like my former math-geek-unbelieving self, Freethinking Jesus shows the logical path to prove that it is illogical to disbelieve the resurrection of Jesus. This was my first book as a Christian so it was published under a pen name, Isaiah Fiftythree.

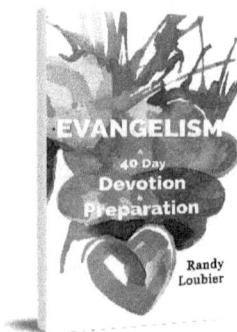

For the long time Christian who is missing the love relationship and needs a spark, this devotional will send you down a forty-day activation path, turning you out of self, toward others. Develop seven habits of living actively in Jesus, walking as He walked, praying as He prayed. This will be the best forty days you've

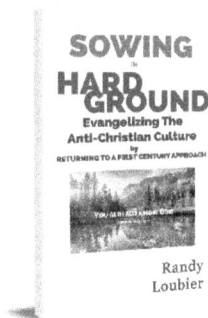

SOWING
HARD
GROUND
Evangelizing The
Anti-Christian Culture
by
RETURNING TO A FIRST CENTURY APPROACH

Randy
Loubier

Do you present the Gospel like Jesus did? Study how Jesus and the apostles talked about the kingdom of God and consider using the Bible to return to a 1st century approach to spreading the good news. Could Christians be contributing to the wave of Western anti-Christian sentiment by ignoring Christ's example?

WHY ARE YOU STILL ALIVE?

# About the Author

Randy Loubier spent most of his life as a businessperson in various industries, starting as an analyst in corporate finance and ending in CEO and Ownership roles.

Spiritually, until age 50 he pursued Asian and New Age faiths and was quite disagreeable with Christianity. At age 50, several events occurred which softened his hard stance, and opened him to a curiosity about the Bible. He picked up a Bible and told God that *if* He was really in it, he wanted to know. He read it cover to cover. It was a Study Bible; he read every scripture and every note, slowly absorbing the message. It wasn't long before he fell in love and was compelled to tell others not to wait like he had.

Today, he pastors a non-denominational church, Chestnut Hill Chapel, in New Boston, NH. His books reflect his sympathy for the "slow brewing tea," the person who is taking a long journey to accept the *full* love of Christ.

He continues to be a voracious Bible reader, passionate about getting God's message right, telling it as Jesus and the Apostles did. To this end, he has strived to remain unaffected by denominations, Christian traditions and trends, and cultural pressure. Just as it is, the Bible brought him to a state of radical joy in Christ and provides enduring wisdom.

For the churched, some might wish to know Pastor Randy's doctrinal bias. With no seminary or church background and his writings nearly devoid of clues, his doctrinal bias is not obvious. Not because it should remain a secret, or that he has not studied such issues as Calvin vs. Arminius, Dispensationalism vs. Church Fathers, pre, post or amillennialism, and other topics, but because he feels doctrinal bias matters not to the mission to which he has been called: helping people find and deepen the powerful joy of saving faith. If you thoroughly believe every word of the Bible, you are a co-servant of the King.

## Notes:

**Notes:**

# Notes:

**Notes:**